The Book of Angela

The Book of Angela

Dedication

The Book of Angela was Written by Angela Smith-Bingham, This book is Dedicated to First and Foremost my Father Which in Heaven and My Lord who sits at the right hand of The Father Jesus Christ into whom I give all Honor, Praise, and Glory!!!

To my Parents Joseph M. Collier III
and my Mother Charlene C. Smith.
To my Godmother Clemtine Jackson
Also Dedicated to My Children
Tasheonia, Johaan, and Anjahlena.

To my late grandmother's
Louise Gaither and Peggy Collier
both who loved me for who I am and
believed in me for all that God called
me to be!!! To All of my Siblings
both natural and Spiritual.. To All of
my Aunties, Uncles and Cousins, and
to all those who have journeyed with
me during this transition and prior.

To All who have helped Give Birth to the Ministry on the Inside of me!!!

To the Pastors Jack Woodard, Bishop Woodard, Bishop Glenn,Pastor Emma Glenn, and Bishop Oglesby!!! To All of the Wives of those Pastors and Bishops!! To All that Read this Book, this is Dedicated to you as Well. I pray that what you learn In this walk that I have walked will be a light, and help you to stay encouraged and dedicated to the Calling God has bestowed on you Today in this Hour.. To God be the Glory Amen.

Introduction

This Book was written in order to document my walk with the Holy Spirit and God the Father. In 2010 I heard God Speak to me in the Thunder and say that I was His Disciple and People would call me

Evangelist so as a Disciple our Father and of our Lord Jesus Christ through the Power of the Holy Spirit it was impressed upon me to write of my experiences in walking with the Father through Jesus Christ and the Holy Spirit. My hope is to Encourage All those God has Called in this Hour to be obedient and endure to the End Amen..

One of many of my testimonies, I was in a car accident in August 2021 that could have resulted in a fatal crash, but because of The Father and His Angels I believe I was saved.. I

told the Lord that day I didn't want
to leave this Earth until I saw the
Fullness.

Satan came for my life through the
accident and through Covid in which
I was two months apart in 2021 but I
give God Glory because He delivered
me and brought me out!!! I
remember I felt like my life was
about to come to an end even after
Covid as if the enemy was trying
hard to take me out, and God put me
on my sister Lavonda Hillman's
mind and she felt the unction to get

to me and pray. While she was trying to call, I was asleep.

When I woke up I was led to call my Dear Sister in Christ and Best Friend Gina. Thankfully God had her already Ready to do what needed to be done, she had been listening to a deliverance program and already had her oil ready. I began to confess to her how I had been feeling. I spoke to my mother and godmother, but nobody really understood or received what I was saying.

I didn't come right out and say how I was feeling, but I said it in a way to try to come off lightly. I tried to tell my boyfriend as well, and he didn't pick up what I was saying. Matter of fact he thought I had completely lost my mind because of all the visions and things that were given at that time. I couldn't rest, I was up and down telling him what the Lord was telling me. I was saying how I wasn't worried about anything. I was focused, and determined to adhere to the call!

After Gina prayed, I instantly felt relief. I knew God heard our prayer and was working on my behalf. I knew I would live and not die! So this Book is to let people know God is Real, our relationship with Him is Real, the things you may be going through right now are Real! God hears your cry, He knows exactly what you are going through.. Whatever God said, That He Will Do!!

The Book of Angela

CHAPTER I

In May 1977 God placed Angela inside my mother's womb, and on February 7th 1978 I was born to my mother Charlene Smith and my Dad Joseph M. Collier III.. Several months later I began to greet people by saying, "Hi" to all family members who decided to talk to me as they ran from me while I spoke back..

That was the beginning of many conversations to come. That's right, I was a talker then later I became even more friendly. So friendly, my teachers would move me around the room, and found that I knew no stranger..

That's what we need in this world today!! "Love," people who aren't afraid to spread God's Love towards others!! Not for selfish gain, but for God's Glory!!

I came into this world loving people!! I had no boundaries as far as people were concerned, to me people were people. I showed love to everybody, but I found out later that everybody, "although they may smile and laugh with you." "Also smile and laugh at you behind your back."

In the process of growing up, I listened to my mother talking about God all the time. One day, she and I had a conversation about God. I asked her how she knew God was Real. Mom replied, "Ask Him a thing, and see if He won't do it for you!!" So, I decided to ask Him for a kitchen set. My birthday was coming up, and that's what I wanted. As soon as I prayed, my Grandpa, "Raymond Gaither" came by to tell me he saw a kitchen set at a garage sale he wanted to get for me. He never came back with the kitchen set, but for me, this was enough to believe, "God Is Real." He actually heard my Prayer, and Answered without delay.

CHAPTER II

Later I began seeing things that
would have me wide awake looking
around. Especially after watching
scary movies, or seeing something I
believed to be scary. I remember
going to the beach and seeing crabs.
I was so afraid of what I saw, I
began seeing crabs crawling
everywhere in the dark. I kept

people up because I started screaming, "the crabs, the crabs!!" Later I would try to sleep, and it sounded like I was in a room full of people all talking at once.

This continued for a while until one day my mom's best friend came into town by the name of Sandy!! We loved when Sandy came into town. She was always so sweet to us. I told her about the voices, and she prayed with me. God delivered me that same night of all the voices, and the scary visions.. The next day, Sandy took my little sister Cindy and I to church that Sunday. I remember this pastor stood talking about God, and how someone needed to come to the front of the church. As soon as he said it, I heard the Holy Spirit say, "go to the front!!" I said, within myself, "but God I'm scared," then I said, "I'll Go if you have everybody come with me!!!" Next thing I knew, the Pastor told everyone to come to the front of the church!! So, everybody headed to the altar.

The closer I got to the altar, the more I began to shake. Next thing I knew, I was at the front of the church speaking in tongues with tears coming down my face. I remember this like it was yesterday. The pastor said, " I don't know why God sent this little black girl (me) to that church!!" Then he called a lady's name and told her to come kneel at my feet while I laid hands on her. I laid hands and prayed for this lady, and later my sister told me what she remembered.. She said, "while I laid hands on this woman and prayed, the whole church began to rejoice." People started shouting and the power of God came into that place!!!

God can use anybody for His Glory!! Including a little child!! No matter the age, or even the gender!! God calls whosoever He Will!!

When I was done praying, she said I began to weep, because I had no clue what just happened.. I didn't understand what I was doing standing in front of all these people.. Afterwards, my sister and I

found ourselves in the arms of
Sandy. She cuddled and held us until
we were comforted.. That was the
beginning of many things to come.

CHAPTER III

My mother, siblings, and I went to Fountain of Life Worship Center Church In Kokomo, In. The Pastor there was Pastor Glenn now Bishop!! Around this time I was unable to have control of my limbs. I began standing up in church saying what thus said the Lord. My grandmother had a couple of addictions at that time. This led her to somehow break her arm!! While in the middle of testimony service I went to stand as I did many times over as the lord led!! Every time my mom would try to set me down!! She had no clue at the time that as much as I tried to sit down, the Holy Spirit would cause me to Stand!! I'd sit, and God, through His Holy Spirit, would stand firm from within to the outside of my flesh!! Whereby, I had no other choice but to "Stand!!"

Living a Life like that, you become very submissive and obedient to the Holy Spirit!!!

It's as if I had no choice but to submit!! Today I'm grateful for that gift and wouldn't have it any other way.. At one time I would question why?? Now I Give Thanks for God using me for His Glory!!! Now back to the story..

 I remember telling my Grandmother, "God said, He's going to Heal you!!" And He said, He's going to deliver you from your addictions too!! As I Spake, the Holy Spirit came upon my grandmother that day!! God rest her soul!! I remember my grandmother began to yell!!! I saw God change my grandmother before my very eyes.. Grandma was healed and stopped everything she was doing, until years later when my grandfather got sick.. I recall God using me to tell my mother about things by dreams of what was going to happen even in her relationship.

God has no boundaries, If you allow Him in, He's able to change every area of your life..

CHAPTER IV

Growing up I had a godmother, mother, and a very special Auntie that helped watch over me and raise me!! These women and I developed a special bond.. My godmother was the one I could talk too about life, and all of its many struggles!! My mother I could always talk to about

God and life as well!! With My Auntie I felt more freedom to be a kid with and as I grew I just stayed close to her.. All of these women had/have very Powerful Relationships with the Almighty God!!! They All Loved/Love God!! They all have had their own encounters with God!! They all were set apart!!! They all went through their own journey with the Lord. Each dealt with rejections with people.

God is So awesome, It's amazing how He places people in your path in order for you to grow in your calling, and in your relationship with Him..

Along my journey I was molested by multiple people, abused physically and mentally, abducted, and raped. These things had a major impact on my journey and In my relationship with The Father.

Some of these things happened by trusting the wrong people. Trusting people is something that came natural for me personally. When I was young I was very naive when it came down to people. I actually thought the people who hung out with me were my friends. I thought everybody that was around me, wanted the very best for me. I wanted the best for people, and had a genuine love for folks. I believed that unless people gave me a real reason not to trust them. I had no reason not to trust people. I thought everybody had good intentions for me and my family. I tried to see the best in people regardless of who they were or what they did.

My cousin Keilee was just the opposite, she didn't play any games. When it came to people, it was as if she could actually read straight through them. If she told me somebody wasn't my friend. Majority of the time, she was absolutely right. She always kept it real with me. Throughout life she always looked out for me as well.. Everybody would always complain because we were so close. If somebody said something about one of us, we hopped right on defense mode..

God is very strategic when it comes to timing. He knows when to put the right people in your life in order to make things happen. In my Journey, I learned how patient God really is. How specific He is about every little thing concerning His Children. I've seen where I was obedient in certain areas and disobedient in others.

CHAPTER V

I recall going to California with my dad, and I asked him to come watch me get on this slide. The pool wasn't like the ones we had in Indiana. The numbers were written inside of the water. I waited until my dad came with me and went down the slide. I found myself drowning. I did what I was taught by signaling people in order to make them aware that I was indeed drowning. I went down the slide, came up, realizing as I tried to plant my feet I couldn't stand in the water.

Like a rock, I began to sink.. I'd swim up to the surface, and with my finger, I signaled one.. I got all the way down to three, and my dad tapped the lifeguard on the shoulder and told the lifeguard, I was in the pool drowning. I was then rescued and vomiting because of the chlorine intake. My dad is a Military man and he was raised, "old school." In an era where they would just throw you in the pool, and assumed you'd swim. So when I asked him, "daddy did you see me drowning." He replied, "yes, I saw you, but I was teaching you a lesson." "I waited until you got to three then I called the lifeguard." I asked, "what was the lesson?" He said, "next time, check to see where the numbers are prior to getting into that side of the pool." I definitely earned and received that lesson.

Daddy wanted me to pay attention. Know what I'm getting involved with before I get into it. If I took this into consideration fully, I would have saved myself a whole lot of heartaches..

I was home one day with my mom, and went to bed with gum in my mouth. Mom always told us, "don't go to bed with food or gum in your mouth." This time I fell asleep chewing gum, and got choked in my sleep. Thankfully, I was in the bed with mom, and she helped me.

Psalms 34:19 of the Darby Bible says Many are the adversities of the righteous, but Jehovah Delivereth him out of them all: I can most certainly say I was hit throughout my life with divers kinds of adversity, but because of God's Grace and His Mercy. He delivered me through them All.

CHAPTER VI

When I was younger, I was carried away with doing whatever. I didn't feel like people believed me when I spoke on how I felt about things. Especially when I tried to declare my innocence. When I would try to defend myself, I had this smirk that would appear on my face. For some reason when things got too serious for me, I would automatically get this smirk on my face. This was a major hindrance on my part, because it was so hard for people to take me seriously. Not only that, but I was falsely accused many times due to it. I received whippings I should have never had due to, "the smirk."

I was very well misunderstood growing up, and at times, I still am. Instead of people asking me, they would automatically assume a whole lot. People have misjudged my character oftentimes due to never coming into an understanding.

People are so quick to judge someone, I believe that's why the Bible says 1Corinthians 4:5 KJV 5 Therefore judge nothing before the time, until the Lord come, who both will bring to light the hidden things of darkness, and will make manifest the counsels of the hearts: and then shall every man have praise of God.

One day I was accused for messing around with a married man, at the time I had never actually physically had sex. So, I told my mother this wasn't true, and I was asked if I was calling the one who told her this a liar. I got in trouble and decided I may as well be having sex, since nobody believed I was a virgin still anyways. I was young and didn't realize that this was a test. It had nothing to do with everybody else and it was a lesson.

The lesson was to not allow my goods to be spoken evil of as it says in the bible in Romans 14:16. See as long as God knew the truth it didn't matter what everybody else said.

I had an issue trusting my gut for the longest time. The Holy Spirit would try to direct me in this way. For some reason I completely tuned out the Holy Spirit. I allowed people to influence me to speak to a stocker who got my number from the bookstore at my school. I was raped for the first time.

I got pregnant with my first child when I was a teenager. I was told afterward I would never have children. During this rape my uterus was torn, and I was told I would never be able to carry children, full term. My dear friend, "Lonnie," told me that she would carry my babies for me. That day I went to the Lord for myself, and I told him I wanna carry my own babies. I prayed and God answered speedily. It came to past that all of my children were born on the 26th, and all of my children's months added up to 26. Twenty six has been a very potent number in my life ever since.

I met my Child's dad's mother Tina, before I met him. She saw me for the first time, at my first talent show, at the Carver Community Center in Indiana. I was all dressed up with my lil sister Cindy, Drikia, and Romeka. I was singing and dancing, "Don't Walk Away" by Jade. While my Sister and our friends danced in the background.. She picked me out of the group, told me I was a pretty little girl, and that she had a son. She asked me my age, and said I was a little too old for him. Later I met her son, and he lied about his age of course. My girl's and I didn't win that talent show that year, but it was fun irregardless.

I later repeated the talent show, but this time with my cousin Keilee. We did it, without all the dancing. This time I prayed first. I asked God to help my cousin Keilee and I to win this talent show. I had a dream later that night, we won First Place. I told everybody, and we won for real!!

CHAPTER VII

After I got pregnant, my oldest sister on my mother's side, Sonsaray, told me she had a dream that the father of my child was abusive to me. I said, "nah I don't think he'd do that." He was actually raised with an abuser, so there's no way I thought he would do such a thing. Only because I believed him when he told me, he would never put his hands on me. Later, her dream became my reality, and eventually I broke it off. I had to break it off, because it became so traumatizing to my daughter. She would wake up and start screaming. One day, I asked myself, do I want my child to grow up believing men are supposed to treat her this way? The answer was no. I decided that day, it was over.

Afterwards, it was as if I never left, because this man continued to come after me regardless. I remember going to church, wearing long dresses, trying to please God. I was even abstinent, yet this young man still continued to attack me. I became upset with God. I started asking Him why He was allowing these things to continue to happen. Why wouldn't He just make this man "leave me alone?" I decided to leave in the middle of my senior year. I was completely embarrassed in High School when we got into a fight in the cafeteria. He spilled this milkshake all over me, and I spilled mine back on him!! I went to Louisiana with my Late Aunt Diane, and met a man by the name of Kevin. I witnessed to this man a whole lot about God.

After seeing my daughter's dad wasn't going to leave me alone. I went back to see Kevin, at that point it seemed as if this man wasn't going to stop attacking me. I decided I would try seeing if maybe things would work out with Kevin and I. This time when I was there, I stayed with him and his mother. I came to help his mother out due to surgery. Kevin asked why I didn't talk about God so much anymore. I told him, "because I didn't understand why God would allow this man to continue to put his hands on me." I stopped messing with him and chose to follow God instead. I just couldn't fathom how he was still able to put his hands on me. I knew my relationship with God. I knew God had absolutely no limits, and that he was bigger than mere man. So how was this man able to put his hand on My God's Daughter!!

Kevin and his mother lived in his late grandmother's home. One night, after speaking with Kevin about the possibilities of my daughter and I coming to stay with him. I fell asleep and woke up to a spirit that came into the room. Kevin had a puppy, and this puppy began barking.. The puppy saw something I couldn't see. I remember the spirit telling him to lay down. Afterwards I remember her telling me ``You'd better go on down that road," I said, "huh?" She said, "I said," "you'd better go on down that road." And the spirit left.

When Kevin got home from work, I spoke to Kevin and told him what the woman said. I also made him aware that I believed it to be the spirit of his grandmother. He told me that she always gave people great advice and asked what I thought she meant by what she said and to listen. Before I left I remember the dog got hit by a car. That was the first time I had an encounter such as this. I knew without knowing that this was this man's grandmother. She was warning me to go on about my business. She obviously knew something I didn't know.

Afterwards, God began dealing with me on the road as I rode the greyhound back to Indiana. I met a woman from Gary Indiana. We spoke about the Lord, and I began telling her about my experience and what was happening in my life at the time. She began to encourage me, and talk to me about what she was doing in the community as a foster mother. During that trip, I spent that time speaking to God. Through this whole experience, I learned how to pray for my daughter's abusive dad. It was as if all of a sudden God showed me how to pray this man away.

See, instead of praying selfishly, I needed to pray for him selflessly. Because, in this man's mind, he really believed he loved me. He didn't understand why I wouldn't take him back. So, he kept attacking

me. Thinking this would cause me to go back to him.

I prayed for God to help this man take the love he has for me, and put it in someone else. Before I knew it, he stopped coming over. Then, suddenly I heard he had a girlfriend. Man, I was so happy that day!!! I didn't have to watch my back any more.. Those days of public embarrassment ceased, because he finally moved on!!

Let this be a lesson, when you are in a situation, that you can't get yourself out of. Pray to God selflessly about that situation. If you have gotten yourself into a trap, and you know this person means you no good.. Seek the lord wholeheartedly about the situation. Consider the other person, and change the way you see things. It's not just about you but God knows that person's heart too.

After God found him someone, later down the line, for a moment I got foolish and almost went back. God brought back to my remembrance that I prayed for that woman. I decided that day, if God delivered me out, I wouldn't place myself back into the same situation twice. That was considered a true entanglement for me, because I couldn't get myself out of the situation. After this situation, God showed me things in dreams even more.

CHAPTER VIII

One day when I came home to my apartment, I was just about to turn the light on, and my daughter began to cry. As soon as I heard her cry, suddenly I began to smell gas. I went to check the stove, and saw it was on. After turning off the stove, a penny was thrown at the television in mid air. Something followed me back from Louisiana and began to come for my life..

Later I got involved with my son's dad. Things went kinda fast between us, He asked me to marry him with no ring, and we got pregnant. When I got pregnant my son's dad started treating me cold heartedly. I left to visit my dad in Virginia. While there I prayed about this baby, and asked God if this wasn't the man I was supposed to be with, to take the baby. When I came back to Indiana, I started this job in a factory. I was at work experiencing heavy cramps and nausea. I tried to get off work early, but I was new and was told no from management. I stayed and on my way home I passed out at the wheel.

I had a 92 Chevrolet Corsica at the time and ran into a brand new Corsica thinking the light was red, trying to stop the vehicle, I ran into the car head on as he was waiting at the light. This man cursed me out, accused me of being on drugs. Not knowing I was three months pregnant, with a dead baby who was deteriorating inside of me. Causing toxins to come into my body, and eventually knocking me completely unconscious.

I asked and God answered, I broke it off with him, only for him to come back this time with a ring. I said yes still, and once again got pregnant. This time with a son. God gave him a dream about the next man after I was a few months pregnant. This would be the one I would marry. I believe this was a warning, giving him the opportunity to get things right before snatching me out of his arms. Next thing I knew, I was marrying the man my son's dad described. He said he saw me marrying a heavy set light skinned man, with green eyes. I wasn't even far enough along to tell the sex of the baby, and he said he saw our son in the dream. When he described this man he saw me marrying, I didn't have a clue as to whom he was talking about. The craziest thing about it was that I actually met this man five years prior.

It was so ironic because for some reason we kept running back into one another. I recall seeing this man when I was young. He went to the beauty school, trying to become a barber. I would go there to get my hair done when I was a teenager. I saw him every now and then, walking around in the area in which I lived multiple times. I asked a few people who this guy was. Most of the people I spoke with had no clue as to who I was even talking about. When my son's dad described him, I had no clue who he was talking about. One day as I was leaving my girl Tisha's house, I saw him. It was as if it was the first time I had ever seen this man. I made a statement and went on about my business. Before I knew it this man was at my door. He came by one day pulled up with a whole Limo. I was like, "What" I didn't know this man was a detailer. Matter of fact I didn't know what he did for a living.

He came by one night and we watched a movie, he kissed my forehead, and left. Years went by, and I actually forgot all about this man. One day this guy I was dating showed up with this man at my new place. We looked at each other surprised, because it had been years. A few more years later I was at the fair pregnant with my son. We ended up bumping right back into each other. He said, "I'll be to see you, after you have that baby." At that time my son's father had decided to go to another state. Claiming he was going to make a better living for us. Later to find out, he was there for himself. My ex husband showed up one day and it was like a movie, or something you would see on one of these talk shows on television. My son's dad was talking to my ex husband's ex, I had just started kicking it with my ex husband. They had actually met over the internet.

I would take my ex husband to the back of this woman's house. At the time he still had his dog there. When it all came out about my son's dad and my ex husband's ex. I kicked my son's dad out of my house, because he was only there claiming he needed a place to stay while spending time with our son. I got a phone call claiming he was in

the park with no place to go asking
if I would just let him come back. I
left my door open all night, woke up
and the man still wasn't there! I was
so upset, because I had children and
left my door open. I got up to take
my daughter to school, and
something told me to go by this
woman's house. Now keep in mind,
I had only seen the back of this
woman's house. I wasn't very
familiar with that particular area. I
never knew this woman, and never
knew what the front of this
woman's house looked like. I went
through the back and saw my baby
dad's car. I drove to the front, and
proceeded to knock at the door. I
made up my mind I was only gonna
tell this man to come get his stuff

and leave. The girl comes out stretching, as I asked for my son's dad.. As soon as he came to the door, "I punched the man in the face." "I kid you not," after my daughter's dad, I became way more short tempered when it came down to silliness.. I was so upset at myself, because I had made up my mind I was just gonna talk. He comes out trying to hold my arms. I walk to the car, to take off with my son. He makes a scene, gets in front of my car trying to force me to stay. I almost hit him with my car.

It was ugly, I admit it. This is the first time I recall having black outs. I would allow myself to get so upset I'd go to do one thing, but instead something else would happen. I didn't know this was a problem, because I never heard people talk about it. I knew it was wrong to put your hands on people. I just didn't know you could black out like that. This has only happened that I can remember a few times in my life. Two of which were because I was upset about the safety and well being of my children. I went there with this man because I thought about the possibilities of what if.. What if something had happened and someone came in and hurt me and my babies. The door was left open all night as a single mother you find yourself having to play the role of protector. I was upset, not because he was with another woman. I was in the middle of moving on with another man. It truly was the, "inconsideration for me."

- **See I was brought up believing that, "we should consider ourselves!" In other words as it says in Matthew 7:12 KJV 12** Therefore all things whatsoever ye would that men should do to you, do ye even so to them: for this is the law and the prophets.

It was the fact that he knew I had children, one of which was his. He still chose to consider himself over his child and our safety. I was always big on safety and most women especially mothers are.

Learning to trust God with your Family is so important. Trust God to protect you and your family. You may not be able to trust a man to do what needs to be done in the role of a father or a man. Just know that you can always trust God. The Bible tells us in Proverbs 3:5 Trust in the Lord with all thine heart; and lean not unto thine own understanding. 6 In all thy ways acknowledge him, and he shall direct thy paths.

Needless to say, "I married the light skinned heavy set man with green eyes my ex dreamt about." My ex husband and I stayed in this house on North Indiana St. We literally saw the living room door open and close in this house. We would literally see the actual door knob turn.

CHAPTER IX

Prior to marriage, I remember I was working out of town in Indianapolis with the mentally ill. I started having feelings of insecurity. I had a Deep desire to go home that I couldn't shake, because I felt as if he was cheating on me. I remember talking to him about it, and told him that before we got married I needed him to tell the truth. I felt as if that were the case we needed to stop everything until we got that right. He told me I was crazy, and continued to lie about the situation. He claimed he had steak and potatoes at home, and asked why he'd wanna replace that for peanut butter and jelly.

One day I saw my friend from school at Walmart and her sister. I heard the Holy Spirit say, "that's her," that's the one he's been sleeping with. It had been a while since I actually heard the Holy Spirit speak to me. It was as if someone was speaking directly in my ear. I then automatically began to reason within myself and said to myself. "No Way!!" I don't even know this woman, there's no way she could know him. I thought, "Maybe I really am going crazy." I proceeded to talk with my friend and told her I was getting married. She asked who I was marrying, I said to this man they call Detroit Ray. The look on her sister's face truly told it all. She began to smirk, because she met me for the first time.

God may be speaking with you about a situation right now, are you listening??

After all of this happened I consulted God, asking if I should marry Him. I did what my mom considered sending out a fleece. In other words, I asked God if he wasn't the husband He had for me. Allow this man to get locked up, let us break up, or if anything like that was to happen I would know not to marry him. Otherwise if everything continued as is, I would know to go through with it.Not long after praying, "He got locked up!" The love I had for him, and seeking the advice of others, I went along with it, and married him anyway.

Once again I had to learn the lesson of listening to my gut. Listen to the Holy Spirit, don't be a people pleaser be a God Pleaser!!

I remember after he and I got married we went to the store. I saw this same woman after only seeing her one time prior to marriage. I knew somehow exactly who she was still! I tried to stop her because I wanted to ask her a question. At that time, my daughter's dad said she was telling people she slept with my husband prior to us getting married. So I asked her if she had been telling people this, she replied, "no!" I then asked, did she sleep with him, which is what he didn't expect. She admitted to sleeping with him, claiming, "only a few times." I told him it was over and we were getting a divorce. Only to call him back home because I found out I was pregnant with his only child.

My dream life really heightened during the time I was married. I really began dreaming dreams so real, I'd wake up in tears!! One day while my ex husband's cousin was in town I had this dream about twins. These twins were strippers, in the dream his cousin introduced them to my ex husband. My ex husband started liking the one his cousin liked and they started having an affair. After my divorce I came across my ex husband's cousin, and he said it blew his mind how this dream came to past exactly how I dreamt it. The marriage came to an end. Before it was over, my sister Meka, "who is gifted indeed," came to the house. She said she saw where someone who lived there prior killed their wife with an ax.

My ex had a dream that I was seeing my ex boyfriend. This was completely impossible because he was in jail at the time. In his head he was out, and we were seeing one another on the downlow. I tried to tell him otherwise until I got fed up and just started laughing. I laughed because I was tired of being accused of infidelity when we both knew who was doing all the cheating. Next thing I saw was something like a scary movie, and I was out.. My keys were taken, my phones were taken, and someone was at the door with an ax.. That was the final straw, I was completely done. The divorce happened so fast, I don't believe either party was truly ready.

Divorce is definitely the last alternative as far as i'm concerned. I never wanted divorce, so I stayed until I couldn't stay any longer. It was truly like death because I went through mourning.. It was very hard to really even comprehend it was over.

Just as his dream showed, I found myself back with someone from my past. My first love, the man I thought I would have married before any other man came along. When that didn't work out I started dating new people. One guy I dated, his phone started calling me back after we would get off the phone. I would get a ring back for some reason. Then I'd hear everything he had to say about me and about the situation he was in. I heard he was a playa and was juggling women, I got myself caught up in the juggle.Another person had the same thing happen, and both stated I didn't hear the part about them considering me to possibly be "The One!!" One of which God even revealed what was going to come with him to my sister Lavonda, before I even knew what all he was into.

Today I realize God was trying to help me avoid some things. Over and over I found myself walking directly into the traps regardless, wasting five years here and there each time.

CHAPTER X

I found myself caught up in a multitude of traps. One of these traps I recall was when my cousin and I went out for the first time together. Prior to this incident I was told by my sister Lavonda because God was really dealing with her at this time. She said God told her to tell me I had my time, now it was his time!! In other words I had my time to do what I wanted to do, now it was time to get about His business. I heard the message and sort of blew it off. While my cousin and I were trying to go out she couldn't find her ID, so many things happened to say no don't go, but ignoring the signs we went anyway.

I remember having three drinks, one of which I remember somebody throwing money in the air. I used that money to get my last drink. We sat at the bar that night, and I didn't watch my drink like usual and needless to say I found myself driving around drugged. It started at the bar when I didn't wanna leave. When we finally left, I stopped at my ex because I forgot how to get to the hotel. I was taken advantage of, and he came out telling my cousin something was wrong with me, and asked her to either drive or for us to stay. At that time, he should've known something was wrong for me to even show up at his place. He tried multiple times prior asking me over, but I would dismiss every attempt because I was involved elsewhere. I came out cussing him out, because I saw him bent down trying to explain why we should stay or she should drive. I didn't know exactly what he was talking about. I got way out of character, and started accusing him of trying to sleep with my cousin. Then I found myself trying to find this hotel again and got a flat tire, and passed out. I remember looking over at her saying to myself, well she's asleep, so I may as well go to sleep too.

I should've known then something was most definitely wrong. While I was knocked out, I was told that this man came to the car and was peeping out what was going on. He came to me then to my cousin then back to me. My cousin woke up and saw him and was trying to ask me what was going on, but I passed out. I woke up to a man I had no clue too, raping me. He made up a whole story saying I left with him and his friend left with my cousin. Like we hooked up in some way and since I woke up, he could then take me to find my cousin. We began looking and finally he spotted her at a gas station in the middle of the night. We got there and they stated they called the police. That man politely got into his vehicle and took off. I was confused, I asked where he was going.My cousin asked where we were, I was like what do you mean and where's his friend. I thought this was something that happened because of alcohol. Then she told me what really happened.

This man claimed he was going to help fix the tire, and told her to drive his car, said for her to follow him as he put me in his car and pulled off. She called my mother, her sister, my siblings, and the police. Everybody was coming down to look for me. I was so embarrassed because I never wanted anybody looking for me due to something like that.. I woke up to a total stranger who abducted and raped me. He lied so I wouldn't go off because I jumped up and asked where my cousin was at!!! As my cousin confronted the man, he hurried to his car and pulled off. This situation had me going consistently before the Lord and this is when Things began to Change!!

My Mother always told us that whatever we didn't learn from her, not to worry, because what she didn't teach us, life would..

Prior to this, I remember looking for a house I was married at the time and I was looking for a 3 bedroom. I looked at this 3 bedroom and it was small. I had been on my own since I was 18 so I was trying to find something big enough for me, my husband, and my three children. I sought the lord and I heard 4 bedrooms 2 bathrooms 2 car garage, I said huh?? I heard the Spirit repeat it again, "four bedrooms, two bathrooms, two car garage!!!"

I began looking even though I was on Hud at the time and my house voucher was only for a three bedroom two bath. I saw the house and I spoke with the landlord. He said that people get that house with that size voucher because the fourth bedroom didn't have a closet door because it was a sitting room prior..

Listening to the Holy Spirit got me this house and set me up for my brand new Home!! My mother was telling me about Habitat which I tried for in the past and for some reason or another it never worked out for me. She said they were looking for people who qualified to apply. I was like mom, I've tried this many times in the past. I didn't wanna do it because it just never seemed to work out for me. Next thing I knew, they called me, and asked me if I was still interested. They had an apostle build coming up and wanted to see if I was interested. They said they had other applicants before me and If they didn't take it I would be the very next build. I told them I was interested, they told me all that it would require. Nobody else wanted it, so I decided to take it.

That same year, God had blessed me with a better Job, a Fairly new Car because the one I had got hit by a Semi, and a Brand New House. Yes, I got hit by a Semi at my brand new job. After coming out of the medical field, working with the mental Ill, I went back into the factory.. People were telling me to apply early on, but I was hesitant, because I knew with the factory jobs. You never knew when you may get laid off.. I applied anyway eventually and was the last group to get hired!! Afterwhile, I was doing overtime and everything one night I was on my way to Bible Study and got hit in my STS 95 green Cadillac by a Semi who decided to start turning Right in the Left Lane! Before I knew it this Semi was embedded on top of my Cadillac. I was able to get out of the vehicle with a scratch. It seemed like after this incident occurred, I ran into many people who had the same experience. Many didn't make it but thankfully God allowed me to be a living testimony!!!

Just that fast, the car I just bought a few months prior was gone!!! Through it all God spared my Life!!! My House was built, I got a Buick Century, and by this time I also had an SUV. I had been laid off from my job after I was about to receive the house. I ended up laid off and having to trust God with my finances and my next move. I remember a lady came to me during this transition. Because of the type of build I was receiving, she saw in the paper. She also knew I just bought a car. She said, "I hear you're getting laid off," "didn't you just get a car and a house built," then proceeded to laugh in my face. I didn't know her, but for some reason she was so intrigued by what was going on in my life. Not knowing that soon she would face the same issues.

Sometimes in life, we can get caught up in what other people have to say about folks. Not knowing

when you put your mouth on others, the same thing can come towards you. "Never laugh at another person's struggle."

 During this layoff, I prayed and asked if I should take the buyout. God gave me a dream that I was going back, and was gonna have greater pay, and things were gonna be better than before. I was laid off a total of three times, the first was about four years. They tried not to allow me and those hired along with me to come back. God allowed me to remember the lady from benefits at the time saying that if we didn't get a call within five years, we would no longer be eligible for call back rights. Because I remembered that information, everybody besides those who received the buyout were able to come back to work.

The Bible tells us in Philippians 4:19 KJV "But my God shall supply all your need according to his riches in glory by Christ Jesus."

In 2012 I was laid off once again, this time not as long. This is the time when the abduction occurred. God began taking me to a higher place in Him. I went to church at what was once Agape Fellowship, which would soon be turned to Great Faith. One sunday The mother of the church told me the Holy Spirit said I have the Gift of tongues!! I knew it was true but I had no clue how to use my gift anymore, because I stopped using it long ago.

Seems like that next Sunday I went to church, got up to get prayer. Mr. Austin at the time before they became Pastor's looked at me and I spat out tongues.. He had his wife come up, Lady Austin, she looked at me and said, "You Said You were tired!" Sure enough, I just said earlier that day I was tired. This time I said it, and it came out in tongues!! She then said, "you ain't did nothing wrong!!" I looked at her puzzled, she said to me, "I said," "You ain't did Nothing Wrong!!!" In my mind I had done and been doing a whole lot of things, "wrong!" That Day my whole life changed, I knew all of the things I had done wrong, yet she looked at me and said to me, "I haven't done anything wrong!!" "My God!!" "What a Beginning!!!" "God had wiped everything Clean!!" Afterwards We had a Women's conference, where we began to go around in circles like they did in Joshua 6 KJV of the Bible "The Wall of Jericho."

We began walking around in a big circle around the sanctuary. I kept stopping, as I felt God's presence all over me. I began to cry, and my cousin Angie began pushing me forward!! Before I knew it I was taken up by the Spirit, and brought to the Front of the altar. I had at least eight inch heels on that day. In my mind, I ran up there, but I was told I actually went backwards up the Altar's steps, and got to the microphone. I had no clue what to say, so I began telling my testimony about the abduction, and about what my sister told me prior. Later, the First Lady of the Church was slaying in the Spirit for a while at the Altar. Church was dismissed and she was still slaying in the Holy Spirit. She said right when everybody was about to leave. "If you want the gift of the Holy Spirit!!" "Don't Move!!!" Everybody stood as if we were in the upper room, and tongues began flowing throughout the room!!! My tongues went from child-like to full

Hebrew.. That fast God had developed my gift, and took me to another level in him!!

You can't miss where you are supposed to be in the Spirit. God Will Elevate you to where exactly you're supposed to be.

CHAPTER XI

I remember going with the Church Family to Detroit, and before I went, I kept feeling a touch on my forehead everyday around the same time. Every time I would wipe my head there would be oil on my forehead. This particular time I remember I went to this Church in Detroit and I heard Angels Singing Free. While the gentlemen played the organ, the Bishop of that church asked a question. He said he didn't know why God still had him here when all these things happened to him to try to take him out. I heard the Holy Spirit say, "tell him, it's because I want him to know the truth."

John 8:32 KJV says And ye shall know the truth, and the truth shall make you free.

Later at church I would be called to pray and speak. Meanwhile, God had me all up in His Word on another Journey. I began to hear him concerning other people. Even heard someone say something in the inside of their heart concerning their husband. I heard a whole conversation between this married couple, that I was nowhere near to be able to hear. Then one night, we had a bad storm. I was asleep on the couch in the living room. I was awakened by lightning bolts that were hitting the ground. As they hit the ground, it seemed as though they were going through the ground into my body. I heard El Shaddai Speak through the Lightning and Thunder for the first time. I heard El Shaddai say; "They will call you Evangelist, but you are my Disciple, and Your House Shall be Called A House of Prayer!!"

At that time I had no Clue House of Prayer was in the Word of God. Isaiah 56:7 and Matthew 21:13. During this time, I was trying to get an understanding because I was in sin, yet God was using me. I saw my ex one night and he was drunk

talking to me about how I loved him.
I knew I loved him when I was
young. I tried to explain that my
love for him was no longer like it
was when I was young. He
continued to plead, meanwhile my
son asked who this man was. I
explained to him, he was a friend
from my past. I then told him to go
to the car as I continued listening to
this man. Suddenly, I began hearing
the Holy Spirit say ever so simply
"No." He went on and on to plead
with me to get me back, and the
Spirit continued the whole time
saying , "No!!"

Later, I found myself downtown
Kokomo, Indiana. I kept going past
this building and it began to pull at

my spirit. Have you ever had this unexplainable nudge, like something pulling at you to go into some place? I kept getting these deep desires to go in there. I had no clue as to why, so one day my Mother and I went. We found out it was a Coffee House that served donuts and breakfast and sandwiches. The man who owned it told me that they had Bible Studies in the back room as he offered me to bring people to have Studies there.

The things of God Will pull you in especially when you find yourself caught up in Him. You'll find yourself going into doors you never thought you'd go into because the

Spirit of God is calling you into these places.

I was floored, I couldn't believe God had opened this Door and had Given me a name prior. We began studying and God began giving answers. He began using us for His Glory at that Coffee House. We got connected to a Healing Room group as well through that experience. We studied with their group for a little while. In this journey, you'll find some things you'll agree with fully. When it comes to people, you'll find out that due to a lack of experience, you won't be able to get an understanding. Proverbs 4:7 tells that in all our getting we ought to get an understanding. When there's no understanding, you'll find yourself misjudged and misunderstood. Therefore, you won't be able to walk together..

Amos 3:3 KJV Can two walk together, except they be agreed?

The group and I began going wherever God led us. Before we knew it, God put us inside of a Church building. I was told by the Holy Spirit that we were only there for a season. The pastor needed to be released from the burden of the building. It became a burden because they bought a new one already, and were having a hard time renting the old one out. We came along and another group came to take it over. I saw it in the Spirit, then it came to past exactly as God showed me. It's crazy how God began touching different minister's hearts. One of which was moving out of town and was trying to make a deal to sell me his old house.. We began fellowshipping at one another's house. Later, we found ourselves at my godsister's Shelter. God gave her a vision and named it Safe Refuge.

It's something about visions, you may see it one way, but as it blossoms, you'll see it transition into the fullness before your very eyes. I think of it as a flower with

lots of layers. The only thing you have to do is be obedient and start.

Before I knew it, we began experiencing whirlwinds coming into the building, bringing people out of their rooms for prayer. The Power of God was most certainly in that place. This is when you see that God truly has a soft spot for the lost.. Most people that ended up at Safe Refuge had drug addictions, and were trying to get a new start in life. The very ones who were considered outcast just like the ones Jesus came to save.

People get so caught up in entertaining one another, patting each other on the back, lifting each other up, but what about the ones that are lost. What about those on the highways, under bridges. Those who have no homes, the ones who come into your churches and you make them sit in the back because of the smell, or the attire.. You may donate to the cause, but what are we doing about it? There are now people standing on the side of the road today to get a hand out. Posing as homeless, having many homes, playing on the hearts of the people. So many cold hearted people in the world preying on the weak. Preying on the broken, preying on the children, preying on the homeless.

The next major thing that happened was I was invited with my Dear Sister in Christ Michelle to a tent Revival on my way back from work. I saw a vision as to what was going to happen at this Tent Revival. I asked the Lord, "So are you saying that you're about to use me to take over this Tent Revival??" The Pastor began declaring He knew there were some David's and some Ester's there because of the ease on the way He was able to preach. I Saw this guy pacing back and forth. I had no clue he was a new pastor, and I asked God what was wrong with Him. God said, He wants the Fullness. I heard the Pastor call out a man in back of me saying He needed Healing and the Spirit said It was His Heart. Then there was another Pastor there and that was the main reason I was there. At the end the Pastor of the Tent began asking people if they had anything to say. I stood, and the Pastor took a while but eventually he called on me. I began to reveal all the things I saw. Then for the main person I began to Speak with tongues and I saw the tongues Hit the Pastor in his Belly. This Man had a heavy weight on His heart, because He was hurt by people. God restored Him that Day.

God will use the very last person you would think He'd ever use for His Glory and for His purpose. To make His Name Great!!! They know

who and what you used to be, "but do they know you now??"

While God was using me for God's House of Prayer, I prayed to the Father for a husband. I believed that in order for me to do His Will Fully, I personally had to be married. I felt this way, because so many people that knew me looked at me in such a way. I felt in order for people not to judge me in that way, I needed a husband. The Holy Spirit told me what I had going on was over, and the man I was involved with didn't even know it. The same night He told me this, the man I was seeing had a dream. In the dream he said he couldn't find me, but he was convinced that he would. Before you knew it, that dream came true. I found myself with someone new as the old man was looking for me and couldn't find me. It was over just as the Holy Spirit said it was.

If you notice, before I would leave someone, each time God would send them a warning. They would actually see me with the next man. I believe this was a warning for them to get it together, and showing God's provision to me knowing now what was to come.

God began to use me in my new situation, by showing me where to touch this man one night. I did exactly as the Spirit Led. I remember Him saying, "Why do you keep touching me!!" Then Last He Yelled, "Stop Touching Me!!" I said to Him, "It didn't feel like me touching you did it?" He said, "No" I said because it wasn't me, but the Holy Spirit said He wanted to touch you. He got up out of the bed and went into the living room. God began showing me our Journey together. He sent people to tell us His Plan for us. One person stated, "He Has to See It, In Order For It To Come To Past!!" One night I began dreaming about a marriage. He said I was speaking in tongues in my sleep. I was so loud that it scared him and he woke me up. I dreamt of a Big Beautiful Wedding, I was Smiling, I stopped everything, and said wait, "but God said this man was my husband." Everything went quiet for a moment, before I knew it we were back rejoicing.

CHAPTER XII

I decided to go to Tennessee with my Job. This was a long life desire to go to Tennessee for some reason.

Later I found I have roots there. I began to talk to God concerning Tennessee. I had people praying about me going. Eventually I spoke with the right people and began the process of heading to Tennessee. I then got off track although I stayed in communication with the Lord, but I started to adventure on my own path a bit. Things I thought were together began to fall apart. Including me, the job I was doing started taking a toll on my body.

One night, I had a dream while off work due to surgery that I was about to go to Kentucky. In the Dream I told the children, welp, looks like we're going to Kentucky. I woke up and told the Children I was putting in for a job in Kentucky. My job later went on Strike, I found myself in Crisis mode. Later Covid hit, and the world was in delay. I found myself in a struggle. Once again I found myself totally dependent on God..

Later, after returning to work, I began driving to and from Kentucky for a season. I found a place in Kentucky, the man I believed to be my husband was also brought to Kentucky. It was crazy how this time even though I put my application in first he was transferred before me.

We found ourselves going through some trials together. One night I found myself on a major Interstate

Highway 65 walking in the middle of the night underneath a bridge. I started trying to flag down this lyft driver who was going past me. The Lyft driver went a little way and stopped finally. I ran to the car and asked for a ride back to my city. The Lyft driver said he couldn't take me where I needed to go, but he would take me somewhere safe. Somewhere that I could call a Lyft, Uber or Cab. The man began asking me why I was out there in the middle of the night. I told him what happened, and the man began telling me how he had just got off work. He said, "I wasn't going to stop because I had a long night already, and was ready to go home." Then he said something that blew my mind, he said, "I wasn't going to stop, but God told me to stop!!"

This was so significant to me because I knew the bible said in Hebrews 13:5 I will never leave thee nor forsake thee!!! God brought forth deliverance in the mist of that whole situation.

I remember God leading me to anoint my boyfriend with oil for three days. Something ended up happening, and what should have caused him to end up in jail. God saved him twice back to back that year. God used me to pray with three people to prevent them from going to prison. God stepped in on their behalf and worked out the situations. One was actually in the middle of a bar and a fight even broke loose around us. I continued to pray until I knew that prayer went through, meanwhile, God covered us that night. During these prayers, God would either show me to either just pray that He would grant them mercy, and favor with the Judge. Otherwise He would give me the Specific Words to pray.

One day, my ex-husband did something that caused him to have to go to jail. I had no clue what he did that night. We were divorced at the time, and The Holy Spirit knew exactly what he did.. He used me to ask him, "don't you get tired of doing something stupid." Leading you right back to jail or something to that extent. The look on that man's face was priceless. I'm sure he asked himself, how does she know?? I didn't but God knows all things!! The next day, he found himself in jail. He told me everything he did that landed him in jail afterwards.

I lost my grandmother, she was one of my biggest supporters. When we would have Studies, grandma would come and participate. She always made her presence known!! Before she passed she asked me to say one of those deep prayers for her one day. Not too far from losing my grandmother, I then lost my dear Auntie. Auntie was there when I needed to get away from my daughter's dad. For that, I will forever be grateful!! Then my godbrother, He was at every building we went to. He too was one of my biggest supporters. He was a man of few words, but when He spoke, those Words meant something! I lost many loved ones along the way. Dear and true to my heart. My godmother's Mother, she recognized I knew the Word and always had positive things to say regarding me. Her Sister who would come out every so often and fellowship. She was supporting me even as a little girl all the way into adulthood. Her Cousin, She opened her home to us when we came to Toledo. She was always so sweet to me and my family. Her Aunt, She opened up her home, allowing us the opportunity to visit with the family my other grandmother who was all of those mentioned prior passed Christmas night.. Her last Words to me was that she loved me just as I was. My Uncle passed before her and made me realize you truly can't take those around you for granted. When they say here today, gone tomorrow, that's such a true statement.

The craziest thing happened when my uncle passed my cousin who was like an Aunt passed the same day. Before she passed she told me she was proud of my cousin Keilee and I. She saw us making it as single mothers in our youth, making it. So many have passed on during Covid. Some young, some old, but we're still Here!! We're Here For God's Purpose, on His Assignment.

2 Corinthians KJV 3:1 Do we begin again to commend ourselves? or need we, as some others, epistles of commendation to you, or letters of commendation from you?2 Ye are our epistle written in our hearts, known and read of all men:3 Forasmuch as ye are manifestly declared to be the epistle of Christ ministered by us, written not with ink, but with the Spirit of the living God; not in tables of stone, but in fleshy tables of the heart.

I was told before my accident and prior to receiving Covid by the Holy Spirit to begin Bible Studying with my Children. I heard the name, "God's House of Healing." I started studying and praying with the children, but wasn't consistent. Later, my mother stated that she heard a prophet say, "if you have a calling, and you don't do what the Lord called you to do that year, they're going to die!!" I can't lie, I heard her, but I kinda blew it off. I figured it wouldn't come to past if you didn't receive the message. Besides, I didn't hear it for myself. It was relayed to me through someone else. It seemed as if after Covid many prophets were standing up. You couldn't really tell who was who's. Because I didn't hear it for myself I couldn't really discern.

After hearing this, I found myself in an accident. 8/10/2021 This man ran the light and T–boned my rental. Prior to the accident I had a rental because I had my car in the shop. Had God not sent His Angels help to turn the car I believe I would have died that day. This man hit me in such a way it should have been a horrible accident. It was to the point where a man on the other side of the road got out of his car and said, "I don't know how you didn't hit me, but I thank God you didn't." He went on to say, "You were supposed to hit me." He said, "I was supposed to be in this accident!"

"How you missed me, I have no clue, but I thank you for it!" I was maybe an inch between his car and mine. During the accident no airbags deployed. I believe if it went the way the devil plotted. I would have hit this man and woman's car that was in the back of the man. It would've hit so hard that I would have gone into oncoming traffic, and Lord knows where I would have landed from there.. After this incident, I was in the back of this car, and we came across an accident. I saw this lady stop her car as we were crossing the light. Take her hand out to do something as if she was snatching, something like a soul snatcher. Rolled her window up, and proceeded on through the light.

On 9/10/2021 I caught Covid Prior to this I was in deep prayer against Covid and I remember as I went to my boyfriend's door I felt faint. I swore I was about to pass out. Right after my son got it going places with no mask and not taking proper precautions. Then everybody in my household got it. At this point, it just seemed as if Satan was trying to take my life along with my family's lives as well.

After I got better I headed to Indiana to spend time with my family. Not realizing people really don't wanna see you after you have Covid. Satan was really attacking my family. In the midst of all this we lost my godbrother, meanwhile my godmother, and god sister were in the hospital fighting for their lives as well. I began going hard for God because I felt like while I was still here I would try to see the fullness of what He placed me here for. I knew He had me Here for Purpose. I tried to tell everyone how I was feeling, because I had that concussion from the accident. When I had Covid it was pretty bad and I was too stubborn to go to the hospital. I didn't feel like I was gonna be here much longer.

I tried to tell people how I was feeling, my boyfriend at the time thought I was just crazy. It went over my mother and godmother's head. My kid's couldn't read into what I was saying to them. I just continued seeking God about what I was feeling.

CHAPTER XIII

I went to Indiana and my sister tried to get to me. She said she felt a unction from the Holy Spirit to get to me, but I was asleep. When I woke up, my mother told me about my sister.. I called my Best friend Gina on my way out of Indiana, and told her I needed to speak with her about how I was feeling. Gina, was listening to a deliverance podcast and was on fire that night. I came and spoke with her about what was going on. She took out her oil and began to pray. She prayed, and prayed until I had to leave. God stepped in that night and I am still here today!! "To God be the Glory!!" I'm grateful to Gina for her obedience to the Lord as well.

As God began to deal with me and I began having three days of Prayer. My godsister, godmother, mom, and Gina was coming together in prayer. My sister Vonda Slipped in, and Michelle came one day. I found myself fasting way more than ever. I found myself praying even in my sleep!! Casting out devils in my sleep!! Speaking with tongues in my sleep. My dreams become even more profound.. Eventually, God created Purposely Designed. I saw myself being able to look into the computer seeing everything that was going on in the spirit in people's homes. I also dreamt about going to this large supplies store to grab everything for the children God assigned to me. As I went I was gathering everything, I wasn't being kind and considerate about it, because I knew the time was short.

Let this be a lesson to you, that Time is Winding up!!

This girl I knew since high school was in the dream. She was mad because she felt I was being rude after I had just told her about a dream God gave me regarding her. I told her I wasn't meaning to come off rude, but time was short, and there wasn't much supplies left. I showed her what I gathered, and told her that she should do the same thing I did, for her children.

I believe in my Heart God has everyone that's still here for purpose. God is still writing the Book, meanwhile we are standing right in the Middle of it. It's not over, but make sure you're in Right standings when it is. See to it that you are being obedient to God's Will in this hour.

I pray for all those who have lost loved ones during these trying times. All who are going through loss. May God visit you, and comfort your hearts. To those having difficulty trying to make end's meet. May God give you strength, as we continue to move forward in this Journey. Look to God as the Bible says in Hebrews 12:2 He is the Author and Finisher of our Faith. Stay Connected to the Vine which is Jesus Christ according to John 15:5. Be fruitful in this Season and make sure you stay in the Will of the Father.

Stay Blessed Forevermore, Amen..

The Book of Angela

The book of Angela is about my intimate journey with the Father. It show's where my Journey began and the different obstacles I faced during this Journey. It speaks on my relationship with others and the things I discovered along the way. It pretty much takes you on my Spiritual Journey, and allows you to see things I went through from childhood into adolescence. These obstacles only touched the surface.

There are more in-depth circumstances in these different difficult trials I experienced.

My hopes are for people to read this book and be able to relate, or get encouragement knowing that God is truly with us and knows all about us. No matter who you are, no matter what you may go through. Take God with you no matter what!! Know that God knows who He called, and through trials and testimonies we are able to help others!! Remember Revelations 12:11 KJV says, And they overcame him by the blood of the Lamb, and by the word of their testimony, and they loved not their lives unto death. Stay in Faith, Don't Lose Hope, You may grow weary, but Don't Faint!! Don't Grow Cold!!! Walk in Love!! Surrender All to God!!

Made in the USA
Columbia, SC
07 August 2022

64398071R00070